"I've taken a few other courses, and then I took Mark's report writing course. Mark's course broke it down better, especially with some of the tips and tricks he brought up. Mark doesn't do the "death by PowerPoint" method of teaching. Mark has his own teaching style, and it is a lot easier to understand. It also really improved my work. Mark pours his heart and soul into his product."

—*Justin Dufault, police officer,*
South Hadley Massachusetts Police Department

"I have taken Mark's online and in-person classes, and the information I have received is invaluable. Mark has shown me how to set up and write a clear and professional report. He makes it simple and easy to understand—not only what needs to be in the report but also the unnecessary things that should be left out. Mark's class has made me a better report writer and a better officer. I recommend Mark's classes to my fellow officers and anyone seeking guidance to better report writing. I am so excited about Mark's book and the invaluable information in it. Thank you, Mark, for making me a better officer for myself and the community I serve."

—*Antoni Hoiby, K9 officer/DT instructor,*
Bristol Bay Police Department, Bristol Bay, Alaska

"Report writing in law enforcement is essential. No other element of our job can be performed within the boundaries of responsibility, liability, or accountability without the profound ability to properly articulate in an understandable format what happened or what is to happen. Mark is an amazing person, one of the best trainers I have met, and has applied himself to an area of practice far too many take for granted. I would urge anyone in the law enforcement profession, as well as anyone who writes reports for any reason, to meet Mark through this book. There is no question his effort in presenting this information will have an effect on any reader's report writing skills. And hopefully, you come to learn who Mark is as he passes on his experience and expertise to us."

—Ben DeHaemers, deputy,
Johnson County, Kansas Sheriff's Department

"Mark's advice and course have greatly shaped my report writing and taken them to the next level. This applies to my role as a police officer and offers a greater understanding of what to look for when I become a supervisor and where I'll look to help shape the future of law enforcement. Thanks, Mark!"

—Andy Garcia, police officer,
West New York Police Department

THE
POLICE REPORT
FORMULA

How To Save Time, Avoid Kickbacks, and Serve Justice Smarter

For Rookies, Officers, Supervisors, and Training Officers

Mark Tagliareni

The Police Report Formula
How to Save Time, Avoid Kickbacks, and Serve Justice Smarter
For Rookies, Officers, Supervisors, and Training Officers

Dedication

To all my fellow police officers and instructors, it's truly an honor to share this great profession with all of you. Your dedication and passion gave me the inspiration to write this book.

To all the people who pushed me and helped me put together my class and this book, thank you. Ben Gioia, your guidance and positivity have been invaluable and have made me a better person. Cherie Woods, your encouragement and time commitment to my PowerPoint and class materials will never be forgotten.

To my family, Evan, Mom, Dad, Laura, Ken, Luke, and Diane, your unwavering support and love guide all that I do.

TABLE OF CONTENTS

Welcome. xi

Foreword xiii

The Dangers of Poor Police Reports. 1

The Challenges of Modern Policing 4

Why This Book. 9

The True Impact of Your Reports. 12

How to Use This Book 15

Police Reports Can Change the World. 19

The 7 Biggest Myths About Police
Report Writing 21

The Police Report Formula (Snapshot). 24

A Quick Hello 26

The Most Important Things In This Book 30

How and Why the Formula Works 37

Step 1 — Patrol Breathing, Muscle Memory,
and Orienting Your Mind. 46

Step 2 — Past Tense, Plain Language,
and the ABCs 51

Step 3 — The Trustworthy and Active Voice . . . 57

Step 4 — Write Like a Journalist, the Use of Force,
and If You Remember Nothing Else . . 60

Step 5 — A Practical Guide to Effective
Police Reports 67

The Art of the Police Report Review 70

Wrapping It Up. 72

WELCOME

Hey, it's Mark.

People ask me what I liked most about being a police officer. In a nutshell, it was the small interactions with people throughout my career. Here's one that still stands out. I pulled a woman over on the highway. We started talking, and the next thing I knew, we were still having a conversation—twenty minutes later! She was a super-cool, interesting person I got to meet, all thanks to my job.

The question came up again when I was speaking at a large law enforcement conference, and it got me thinking more deeply. I loved being a police officer because it gave me the privilege of having all kinds of interactions with people, the kinds that most people don't even know exist. They can be funny, heartwarming, heartbreaking, terrifying, fulfilling, and the list goes on. If you're in law enforcement or a similar calling (it's definitely a calling), you know what I'm talking about.

So, I'm grateful for all of it. I'm grateful for the trust I've been given from the people I've served—and to tell the stories in my police reports. It's been a great way to keep these moments alive in my heart and in my mind.

Police reports can change the world.

I'd love to hear about some of your favorite stories and interactions in this wonderful calling that we share together! I invite you to visit me at PoliceReportFormula.com.

Warmly,
Mark

P.S. Be sure to visit PoliceReportFormula.com and click on "Subscribe" or scroll to the bottom of the homepage and fill out the "Subscribe Form." By providing your email address, you'll have access to writing tips, tools, and a growing community of law enforcement contacts.

FOREWORD

It's my honor and privilege to welcome you to *The Police Report Formula*. This book is the best guide for mastering the art of police report writing because it transforms what many officers see as a dull task into a powerful tool for justice.

And I should know.

Law enforcement isn't just a job—it's a calling. Most of us are here to make a positive impact, to serve, and to protect our communities. Throughout my career in law enforcement, I've faced multiple challenges. As a Latina woman, sometimes, it's been quite a ride—but a ride worth taking because I've been able to help many people and touch many lives.

It's not just on the streets; it's also on paper. Every detail of every interaction is crucial for our reports; each one can mean the difference between justice served and justice denied.

Why is good police report writing essential? Because it's the official record—the backbone of our work.

Memory alone won't suffice.

For example, I am a defensive tactics expert and use of force instructor. So, reports, especially those involving the use of force, must paint vivid pictures. They're our shield against lawsuits and our legacy for years to come.

Throughout my career, I've witnessed firsthand the impact that well-crafted reports can have on cases, investigations, and community safety.

There are times when police reports literally save lives, while "bad" reports can easily lead to lawsuits, lost jobs, and lost lives.

In an ideal world:

- Law enforcement operates without politics.

- Media headlines are objective rather than sensational.

- Every officer has a dedicated training budget.

- Policing is a white-collar profession.

- Well-trained, physically fit officers uphold the highest standards.

However, the world isn't always ideal.

That's why this book is such a blessing. Written by my good friend and brother in blue, Det./Sgt. Mark Tagliareni, *The Police Report Formula* makes it easy to champion the importance of continuous learning for officers, not to mention the hands-on teaching you'll find in the following pages.

Mark's book helps officers navigate the less-than-ideal challenges by teaching them to write straightforward and fact-based reports that are aligned with an officer's purpose, or "reason why."

It also gives field trainers, heads of training, and report writing instructors an elevated approach that looks at the bigger picture, recognizes the human behind the report, and transforms law enforcement.

Mark is a successful and seasoned law enforcement veteran with twenty-seven years of experience. He has guided me as a police instructor and has become a trusted friend.

Not only does Mark share his wisdom in this book, but he also regularly teaches in-person and online classes about effective police report writing.

The Police Report Formula isn't about drudgery; it's about storytelling. As a result, your reports will bring clarity, truth, and humanity to the forefront.

Imagine writing with ease and purpose, knowing your words matter, and serving justice better.

Let's take a smart approach to policing—one report at a time.

I invite you to join me on this journey.

—Lieutenant Elia Alfonso, shift commander, defensive tactics program manager, Use of Force Instructor, Manassas Police Department

1

THE DANGERS OF POOR POLICE REPORTS

In the fast-paced world of law enforcement, clear, concise, and accurate police report writing is more important than ever.

This is a book about effective police report writing. It's a skill and practice that can be glossed over, yet it's crucial to the safety and success of law enforcement officers, trainers, the communities they serve, and society as a whole.

If you're like most law enforcement officers, this may sound like a boring topic. It may even strike fear in your heart. You may be wondering how report writing can be interesting.

In a profession where every detail matters, police reports are often a lifeline; they're not just paperwork.

- Police reports can (and have) literally saved lives.

- Good reports lead to less stress, improved job satisfaction, and better performance.

- Better job satisfaction and less stress lead to improved mental health for officers.

- Being in the best possible frame of mind makes your job safer and more secure.

There was even a situation regarding a potential assassination—more on this later.

The Police Report Formula was developed as I wrote thousands of reports throughout my twenty-seven-year law enforcement career. I have consistently earned praise as a strong communicator and report writer. The Formula will help officers, supervisors, report writing instructors, and heads of training/academies learn an easy and effective way to write best-in-class reports.

Bad police reports can kill people.

No joke.

For example, in 2008, the United Kingdom's Inspectorate of Constabulary found that sergeants spent 45 percent of their time on paperwork. The trend is similar in the United States. The typical police report can take up to two hours to complete (nuance.com pamphlet).

That takes officers off the road and makes their respective jurisdictions less safe.

Think of a report sent to Child Protective Services that is not detailed enough. Will the child referenced in that report get the type of services they desperately need? Will they be safe?

Poor reports lead to cases being significantly down-graded or dismissed outright. In some cases, the result can be legal action against the officer, the department, and/or the city.

2

THE CHALLENGES OF MODERN POLICING

Call volume is up, and manpower is down for most officers across the country. Officers often go from call to call with little downtime. You may be experiencing this right now. This can quickly lead to burnout, or worse, it can lead to mental health issues.

Little, if any, time is devoted to training in any area. We've all witnessed what happens when officers are thrown into the job, not knowing what's expected of them. When was the last time you took any type of training on report writing? Possibly, it was at the basic police academy.

Supervisors spend about 45 percent of their time doing paperwork. This includes correcting subordinates' reports. They miss out on valuable time in the field and guiding their officers.

It is my hope and intention that this book (and my courses and workshops) will help fill that gap by giving officers and trainers the tools they need to write high-quality reports faster and more easily than ever.

Great reports lead to great results. They help reduce stress, save time, and even save lives. By understanding how to include essential details and avoid the biggest mistakes, officers, job satisfaction, job performance, and industry success will improve.

TECHNOLOGY VS. STORYTELLING

You need to tell your story correctly, regardless of the available technology.

Why? Because news comes (almost) instantaneously. People form opinions with only a fraction of the details. The public is often misinformed, or they have misperceptions about law enforcement due to what's reported on TV or through various social media sources.

There are cameras everywhere, including the cameras you wear on your uniforms or have in your police vehicles. These are great tools, but are you relying on them too much to tell your story in your reports?

I've reviewed numerous police reports from all over the country. I am certain some officers are relying far too much on their body-worn cameras (BWC) or mobile video recorders (MVR) to tell the story. You'll be able to access examples later.

WHY BOTHER?

We've all witnessed officers dealing with these challenges and frustrations, or maybe you've experienced them firsthand. It's understandable why some officers ask, "Why bother?" when it comes to report writing.

Here are some reasons why we should bother. Poorly written police reports can have serious consequences:

- Legal implications such as conviction challenges, suspects going free, or civil suits against you and the department.

- Career implications include a poor reputation, weakened credibility, and lack of advancement. Officers who have been discovered as inaccurate or untruthful (purposefully or not) will face significant challenges when on the stand or never be allowed to testify at all.

- Unsuccessful convictions for violent criminals, murderers, rapists, and drug smugglers.

GREAT REPORTS BRING GREAT RESULTS

If you're reading this, you are possibly struggling with writing itself.

Or maybe you're struggling with which details to include in your reports.

Perhaps you're a report writing instructor who is struggling to find an effective way of teaching such an important topic.

While report writing can't solve all the problems I mentioned above, accurate reports can go a long way in transforming misperceptions and making some of these issues more manageable. Keep reading to discover what happens when you know how to write a properly detailed report in an efficient manner.

Here are nine results you can expect:

1. You will learn how to avoid grammatical errors, misspelled words, and commonly misused words and phrases.

2. You will learn which details are important and need to be included in your reports.

3. You will have less stress when it comes to report writing and be more satisfied with your job overall.

4. You will save time, have more job security, and, yes, even save lives!

5. You'll notice you can write reports more quickly and efficiently because you have all the tools you need to do so.

6. Your work becomes more fulfilling because you enjoy it, do your job well, and document your good work properly.

7. You learn how to communicate with people better, not only at work but also in your personal life.

8. Others around you start to notice and decide they want to emulate your work. Passion is contagious.

9. Your improved level of work and properly detailed reports help lead to career advancement.

Police reports are something you do every day you go to work. No matter your job title, job function, or the unit you're in, you will be writing reports. I'm passionate about this topic of report writing because I've seen the outcomes of effective reports. These outcomes can be simple, or they can be epic—outcomes like saving a life, making a crime victim feel safe, and obtaining convictions for murderers, rapists, or drug smugglers.

Now, imagine your life when your reports are a breeze:

- You're able to do them more efficiently and accurately.

- You get your reports correct the first time with no significant editing required.

- You obtain convictions that are agreeable to you and the crime victim (if any).

- You now have a more effective way to teach this topic to those officers in the basic police academy or attending in-service training.

This book will help you do your work completely, get all the proper details, and then tell your story easily and efficiently so you can serve justice better.

3

WHY THIS BOOK

This book is for officers who struggle with easily writing effective reports, as well as instructors looking for a more effective way to teach this critical skill. It's for officers who want to make a difference and communicate better and for supervisors who want to spend less time reviewing reports. It's for training officers and heads of academies who want to make sure officers are writing correctly at every phase of their careers. Simply put, it's an essential tool for every officer who wants less stress on the job and in their personal lives.

If you're like me, you want to make a difference at work. As a police officer, you are in the extremely fortunate position of being able to do this every single day. Early in my career, I realized I could make a difference with my actions. I also realized that I could make a difference with my words.

Being able to make a difference with your words requires attention to detail.

- Details like how someone is behaving.

- Details like the words someone is speaking.

- Details like the way you are feeling in certain situations.

- Details like using the right words to express exactly what took place.

FROM OBSERVATION TO DOCUMENTATION: A COP'S GUIDE

Back when I was new to the force, I stumbled upon a moment that really made me think. I was out with my sergeant on a call about a car that kept popping up parked along the highway. The driver, a woman, seemed to be in a rough spot, and something about her just didn't sit right with me.

She was standing way too close to the traffic, lost in her own world, not even glancing up as we pulled up behind her with our lights flashing. My sergeant was all about figuring out if her car had broken down, but I had a gut feeling that the car wasn't the issue—it was her. Turns out, I was right. She was thinking about ending her life right there on the highway.

That day stuck with me. It made me wonder why no one else had noticed her before and why my sergeant didn't pick up on the same things I did. It got me thinking about all the little details we might be missing daily.

Maybe other officers had seen her but hadn't thought much of it, or maybe they noticed but didn't write it down. Whatever the reason, it was clear that we needed to be more than just enforcers of the law. We needed to be observers, listeners, and, sometimes, lifelines.

From then on, I made it my mission to pay more attention to the small stuff—the things that might not seem important at first glance but could mean everything to someone in crisis. It's a lesson I carry with me every day, reminding me that sometimes, the most important thing we can do is simply take the time to understand what's really going on.

4

THE TRUE IMPACT OF YOUR REPORTS

Let's talk about turning those struggles into victories. I've had my fair share of challenges, like dealing with supervisors who weren't up to snuff and an administration that didn't exactly cheer on proactive policing. I quickly learned that my reports had to be spot-on to avoid giving them any ammo to use against me.

Imagine transforming your struggles into success stories, just like these officers did:

- There's an officer from Mississippi who was making quality arrests but needed to improve his reports. Now, one of his reports is being used as a teaching tool by FBI instructors at Quantico. Plus, he's been moved to the Investigations Division and is cranking out detailed reports left and right.

- Then, there's the officer who learned English from watching cartoons and had a tough time with grammar and phrasing. Now, he's writing with confidence and no longer stressing about it.

- And let's not forget the officer from Kansas who was struggling to put together a report-writing training program for his department. He found the inspiration he needed, and now, he's teaching his colleagues the ins and outs of top-notch report writing.

These are real stories of officers from all over the country who I've had the pleasure of teaching. They've learned the same things you're about to dive into. Get ready because you're on the brink of some game-changing discoveries.

DETAILED DOCUMENTATION WILL MAKE A DIFFERENCE

You have the power to make a real impact, starting right now. And guess what? It's not as hard as you might think. Whether you're wrestling with grammar and spelling or dealing with something like dyslexia, there's hope for you to see some big improvements—and fast.

Ever find yourself wondering if your reports are too detailed, not detailed enough, or just can't figure out what details to include? You're about to learn how to paint the perfect picture for your readers, making sure they get the full story every time.

And if you're having trouble picking up on behaviors, actions, and words, don't worry. You can sharpen those skills, and it will make a huge difference in your safety on the job.

It's all about crafting reports that matter.

5

HOW TO USE THIS BOOK

What you'll find in the following pages can be applied to your overall outlook on policing, not just report writing. Yes, a book on police report writing can also make you a better officer, make you safer, and help you make a difference every day.

Understanding your purpose isn't just a part of the job; it's the backbone of everything you do in law enforcement. When you strap on your badge and step out the door, you're not just going to work—you're answering a call to serve and protect. This sense of purpose drives your actions, informs your decisions, and strengthens your resolve in the face of challenges.

As a police officer, knowing why you chose this path can keep you grounded, especially during tough times. It's not just about following procedures or meeting the expectations of your role; it's about connecting to the deeper reason behind each task, whether you're directing traffic, responding to a distress call, or solving complex cases. This connection not only enhances your effectiveness but also ensures that each decision you make is anchored in justice and community trust.

Your purpose can also be a powerful shield against the burnout and stress that often come with the badge. It reminds you that your work has a significant impact on the safety and well-being of your community. With this understanding, you approach each day not just as a job but as a vital contribution to the society you've sworn to protect.

Moreover, this sense of purpose fosters resilience. When the days get long, and the challenges mount, remember why you started. This reminder can renew your energy and focus, helping you navigate through the toughest days with determination and clarity.

So, take a moment every now and then to reflect on your purpose. Remind yourself that you are part of something larger than the daily routine. You are a crucial pillar of your community, a protector, a peacekeeper, and a vital enforcer of the law. In understanding and embracing your purpose, you not only enrich your career but also enhance the lives of the people you serve.

Furthermore, by understanding your purpose and taking moments to reflect, you will be a safer, more competent officer. We not only serve our communities, but we also serve our families. Going home safely after each shift is our ultimate purpose and goal.

WHAT TO EXPECT FROM USING THE POLICE REPORT FORMULA

When I speak with officers who have taken my class, I hear how their reports have gotten much better and their supervisors have taken notice. They tell me that the Formula helps them write more easily and efficiently. They feel more confident writing reports and know what details are important and which ones to leave out. These same officers and others who have yet to take my class express the desire to see examples of actual police reports. I get it; I learn by seeing how things are done, too.

I invite you to use this book to motivate yourself during those times when your motivation may be waning. Use this book to help you realize that your job is important and you have the ability to change lives. You never know what kinds of calls you'll go on each day. By following the Formula in this book, telling the stories of those calls will come more easily.

By applying the following techniques, you'll be an officer others seek to emulate. You're about to discover a perspective that will make report writing easier and more efficient for you and will make your job more satisfying.

This isn't like any other book on police report writing that exists. You'll find motivation to be more thorough and complete in all aspects of your job, and the rewards that follow when you do will be amazing. What I'm offering is a framework to become a better, more well-rounded officer and then tell your story in a properly detailed report.

By following the Formula, here are the outcomes you can expect:

- You will be writing reports with more ease, confidence, and efficiency.

- If you're a supervisor, you will spend less time reviewing reports and more time out in the field providing guidance to your officers.

- If you're a report writing instructor, you will have a new tool to teach officers a topic that is often overlooked or not given the significance it deserves.

- If you're the head of an academy or head of training, you will have a book that police recruits and veteran officers can use to shape their reports and their careers.

6

POLICE REPORTS CAN
CHANGE THE WORLD

No, it's not hyperbole.

Imagine stepping into a world where every law enforcement officer writes detailed and complete reports with ease. Picture the ripple effect of positive change that would occur if report writing was no longer seen as a chore but as a crucial part of the job.

As someone deeply passionate about law enforcement, I believe that understanding the interconnectedness of all aspects of our work is key to success. When you grasp the bigger picture, everything starts to fall into place, and report writing becomes a natural extension of your commitment to your role.

I'd like you to picture going to work each day armed with the confidence to perform your duties effectively. With a fresh perspective on the importance of report writing, it won't be a struggle anymore. Instead, it will be a powerful tool in your arsenal, allowing you to document your incredible work accurately and comprehensively.

Imagine the impact of your dedication spreading like wildfire. Your colleagues will take notice and begin to adopt similar practices, leading to a collective shift in your department's approach to report writing. As this positive change spreads, officers from other areas will catch wind of the success and start implementing these improvements as well.

Does this scenario seem too good to be true? I assure you, it's not. I've seen these kinds of transformations firsthand. Working with one of the most popular law enforcement training companies in North America, I've been inspired by the countless officers who've shared their stories of making a difference every day. Our company, which started small, now reaches approximately 10 percent of all law enforcement officers in the US and Canada, with over 100,000 followers across various social media platforms.

By embracing the significance of your role and recognizing the impact you can make, you'll approach each call with a renewed sense of purpose. You'll become more thorough, capture all the essential details, enhance your safety, improve your communication skills, and become an exceptional report writer. This book is your gateway to a new era in law enforcement, where officers, trainers, and supervisors are better equipped, more effective, and well-rounded.

7

THE 7 BIGGEST MYTHS ABOUT POLICE REPORT WRITING

You're in a position to make a real difference through your police reports and what you discover here in *The Police Report Formula*. It's not just about filling out forms; it's about potentially saving lives, reducing stress, and increasing job satisfaction. Let's debunk some common myths and set the record straight:

Myth #1: No one will read this report.
Reality: While not all reports are read, some will be crucial. These could be the most important words you write in your career.

Myth #2: This case will be thrown out or downgraded, so why bother?

Reality: Many cases are downgraded, but a well-written report can lead to a plea bargain that's satisfactory for all parties involved.

Myth #3: I can just copy and paste from another report or use AI to write my report.
Reality: Every situation is unique. It's essential to write each report from scratch based on your firsthand knowledge.

Myth #4: I struggle with English, grammar, and spelling or have a condition like dyslexia, so I can't improve.
Reality: Improvement is possible. Tools like Grammarly, MS Word, and Google Docs offer suggestions. For dyslexia, try writing in a program with a pastel-colored background, using a more readable font, and increasing line spacing.

Myth #5: I should be vague with details in my reports to prevent attacks from defense attorneys.
Reality: Include all pertinent facts. Omitting important details can be more damaging if a defense attorney notices the gap.

Myth #6: I'll rely on my mobile video recorder (MVR) or body-worn camera (BWC) to tell the story.
Reality: While MVRs and BWCs are valuable tools, they don't capture all the details. Your report should fill in the gaps.

Myth #7: Reports can't save lives.
Reality: They absolutely can. Your presence and documentation will make a significant difference in people's lives.

Remember, effective police report writing is crucial for documentation, investigations, and serving as evidence in court. In today's climate of transparency and accountability, your reports are more important than ever.

8
THE POLICE REPORT FORMULA (SNAPSHOT)

*T*he *Police Report Formula* is a game-changer for law enforcement officers who want to improve their report writing skills. It addresses common issues like grammar mistakes, unclear terminology, and the challenge of deciding which details are most important. This Formula is not only for officers but also for supervisors tired of sending reports back for revisions and training officers looking to instill effective writing habits from the start of an officer's career.

I created this Formula after years of experience and writing thousands of reports. It's designed to reduce the time you spend in front of a computer screen, increase your time on the streets ensuring safety, and lead to satisfying outcomes in court.

The key to this Formula is using plain, simple language that anyone can understand, whether it's a juror, your supervisor, or an attorney. You'll learn how to write reports that are clear and concise, making your job easier and more efficient.

Here are the five steps to writing consistent and complete reports:

Step 1. Orient Your Mind: Stay present and focused at work to be a safer, more professional, and more complete officer.

Step 2. Past Tense and Plain Language: Consistently write in the past tense and use clear, straightforward language, avoiding unnecessary or overly formal words.

Step 3. Proper Voice: Shift from writing in the third person to the first person, and use an active voice to make your reports sound better and easier to understand.

Step 4. Be Like a Journalist: Stick to reporting the facts. We'll discuss the nuances of including opinions in reports later.

Step 5. Put It All Together: You'll be surprised to find that the format required for police reports is similar to the writing structure you've been using since grade school.

By following these steps, you'll be on your way to writing efficient and effective reports that make a positive impact on your work and the safety of your community.

9

A QUICK HELLO

Hi! I'm Mark Tagliareni. During my career, I've learned that writing effective police reports is not just about following a set of rules. It's about understanding the impact of clear communication and the role it plays in law enforcement. When I developed *The Police Report Formula*, my goal was to address common challenges officers face, from grammar struggles to determining which details are most important.

One thing I emphasize is the use of plain, simple language. This approach ensures that anyone who reads your report, be it a juror, supervisor, or attorney, can easily understand what happened. It's about making your report accessible to all and removing any barriers to comprehension.

- I'm a retired detective sergeant and report writing instructor. I help officers, fellow instructors, training officers, and heads of training academies by offering a simple and easy Formula to help write best-in-class reports.

- I teach a report writing class and have run report writing seminars for thousands of officers from all over the world.

- Among many other invitations, I was invited to teach at the NJ Law Enforcement Youth Academy and delivered the closing talk at a law enforcement conference with over one thousand attendees.

- I was valedictorian of my police academy class, and I hold a master's degree in education from Seton Hall University.

- I was the most successful interdiction officer in my department's history, and I made hundreds of arrests over the course of my career. Early on, I realized the importance of a factually detailed report in garnering convictions for those arrests.

I developed *The Police Report Formula* thanks to writing a lot of reports while in school and at work, getting feedback from other successful officers and assistant prosecutors, taking a lot of training through-out my career, having a father who is a retired English teacher, and having a lot of different experiences at work. Most importantly, the mindset that is Step 1 of the Formula kept me safe and made sure I was doing my job completely. By following the Formula, my reports were always complete, written efficiently, contained the proper details, and guaranteed that justice was served smarter.

WHY THIS IS IMPORTANT

It all started with a young man running down the sidewalk as if his life depended on it. Dressed in nice clothes and carrying a backpack, he didn't seem to be in trouble, but something about the situation piqued my curiosity. When I circled back to talk to him, I discovered he had lost something very valuable to him and his family. Helping him retrieve it turned into one of the most rewarding experiences of my career, leading to a TV appearance and a heartfelt letter from a family halfway across the country. It made me wonder how many officers might have driven past without a second thought.

I've always taken pride in my work, especially when it comes to putting criminals behind bars. I understand that not everyone shares my enthusiasm for writing, but I want you to think of your reports as a reflection of yourself and your work. A well-written report can save you hours in front of a computer, reduce the number of reports kicked back, and lead to more satisfying outcomes in court.

Writing has always been a passion of mine, as has my commitment to my career and fellow officers. Early on, I recognized the importance of police report writing, and now I have the opportunity to share that knowledge and passion with you. My hope is that through this book, you'll come to see report writing not as a chore but as a vital part of your job.

Motivation can come from various sources. For me, it was initially the fear of administration. I enjoyed being proactive, but my department's top administrators and some supervisors were not fans of that approach. I had to ensure my reports were detailed enough to keep me out of trouble. No matter what motivates you, understanding the importance of a properly detailed report is key to success in your career.

Thank you for picking up this book. My goal is to share the tools, techniques, mindset, and motivation that made report writing easy, efficient, and rewarding for me. If there's one thing to remember, it's to always show up to work with the right mindset. By handling every call completely, you'll gather all the necessary details for your reports, enhance your safety, and better serve your community.

10

THE MOST IMPORTANT THINGS IN THIS BOOK

If you remember nothing else, remember this: Always show up to work with the right mindset. By doing so, you will handle every call completely. This will ensure you've gotten all the right details you'll need for your reports. More importantly, it will make you safer and keep those you are serving safer, too.

(If you haven't noticed, I talk about mindset all throughout this book.)

I guarantee that if you show up every day with the promise to yourself that you will handle every call completely, all the rest will fall easily into place. We have all witnessed or worked with officers who don't show up this way every day. As they handle one call, they are already thinking about the next call or something completely unrelated. Are they being as complete as possible? Or worse, are they being as safe as possible? Most likely, they are not. I'm quite sure their reports reflect how they act while at work.

Once you realize that everything is connected and interrelated at work, you will see the big picture. It's been said that you should begin with the end in mind. This couldn't be more true when it comes to report writing. Keep the end in mind as you're handling each call. Ask yourself, do I have enough details to write a truly complete report? Do I have all the elements of the crime in my report? Do I have enough to secure a conviction? If the answer is no, keep asking the right questions and getting all the details until the answer is yes.

A POTENTIAL ASSASSINATION

In the summer of 2016, The Secret Service asked for a copy of one of my reports. It was about a young man named Michael whose car had a flat tire. As I spoke with Michael, I quickly realized he was in crisis (sound familiar?). I convinced Michael to come to our headquarters, where he could be psychologically screened. About a year and a half later, Michael showed up at a Donald Trump rally and tried to assassinate Trump. When I heard The Secret Service had my report, was I worried it was lacking? No. I knew that I had gotten all the right details and asked all the right questions the night I met Michael.

Again, I'll ask: Do you know officers who may have pulled up to a car with a flat tire and only focused on the car? Be more thorough than that. Ask questions. Get all the details. You'll be amazed at how easy it is to write a properly detailed report more efficiently and in a timely manner.

Let's Stay In Touch

We are all busy both at work and at home. *The Police Report Formula* was designed so you can read it straight through or in bite-size chunks. Whichever way you choose, once you finish it, I ask that you stay in touch with me and seek to continually learn. Be sure to follow me on social media so you can get the latest updates, and check out PoliceReportFormula.com

I have a section on networking coming up shortly. By joining *The Police Report Formula* community, you'll immediately see the benefits of networking. By surrounding yourself with the right people and the best sources of information, you'll be setting yourself up for continued success in your career. And don't worry, *The Police Report Formula* community won't just be about report writing. You'll find ways to get answers to a lot of law enforcement questions, and you'll find inspiration and motivation every day.

How To Get the Most Benefit

Share and recommend this book to others in your department or brother and sister officers you know at other departments. Follow me on social media, and check to see when I'm teaching in your area. I'd love to see you in class and meet you in person. If I'm not scheduled to teach in your area, ask your training officer or head of training to host my class. Host departments get free seats in class.

You can access sample reports on my website: PoliceReportFormula.com. Once you're vetted as a law enforcement officer, you can join the Report Sample Sharing Hub, where you can access sample reports for a variety of call types. As a result, you will be more confident writing reports for every type of call you encounter.

If you're not an active law enforcement officer, you can still subscribe to my mailing list. Visit PoliceReportFormula.com, click on "Subscribe," and enter your email address to join the mailing list.

I'm honored to be able to share this career with you and humbled you picked up this book to learn how report writing can be easy and efficient and can change lives.

THE POWER OF NETWORKING

I once had a training officer reach out to me because he was training a rookie who was struggling. According to the training officer, the rookie was being made fun of due to his report writing. This rookie was down on himself due to his poor writing skills.

In the meantime, the training officer had just signed up for the on-demand version of my class. He asked if the rookie could take his spot instead because the rookie didn't have a lot of money and needed to buy some furniture for his house. Since taking the class, the training officer is happy to report that the rookie's sergeant told him the rookie's reports have drastically improved.

That's just one example of networking.

Networking is critical, and it's a game changer—not only in law enforcement but in any endeavor you undertake. I network and connect with people on multiple social media platforms. I'm constantly blown away at how quickly posts are answered. I see officers asking questions that start with, "This is pretty obscure," or, "I'm pretty sure no one will have an answer for this." And guess what? Not only are the questions answered, but there are several helpful answers.

People ask me a lot of questions or send requests for help with report writing (and lots of police matters, to tell you the truth). I am always happy to help or at least point them in the right direction. Don't hesitate to reach out to me on my website PoliceReportFormula.com. You'll find my email address and all my social media handles there.

The book you're reading is a great resource. I recommend you keep it in your duty bag (or available on your phone) and refer to it when needed.

However, books only go so far. In-person training is one of the most valuable ways to learn. So, I invite and encourage you to take my next class.

What I offer is engaging and different from any training out there. Just ask the chief in Constantine, Michigan. After class, he kept telling the officer in charge of training how good the training was and said they'd never had anything like it there before. I can't wait to go back to Southern Michigan!

Watch Out For "One Size Fits All"

When it comes to report writing, one size certainly does not fit all. This was clear in a conversation I had with an officer from Mississippi who almost enrolled in a report writing course that advocated only for a singular writing style. Thankfully, a friend told him not to do it, and he took the advice.

Report writing can be approached in various ways. Each officer has their unique writing style, and it's important to recognize and embrace this diversity. The idea of forcing officers to conform to a single style of writing is not only unrealistic but also counterproductive.

THE POLICE REPORT FORMULA IS A TOOL THAT RESPECTS THIS DIVERSITY.

It provides a framework that can be adapted to different writing styles, ensuring officers can write reports that are clear, concise, and effective while staying true to their voice.

By using this Formula, officers can improve their report writing skills without the need to drastically change their writing style. This approach makes the writing process more natural for officers and leads to reports that are more authentic and easier to understand.

When it comes to report writing in law enforcement, flexibility is key.

If you keep reading this book and put what you learn into practice, here's what will happen:

1. You'll notice you can write reports more quickly and efficiently because you have all the tools you need to do so.

2. Work will become more fulfilling because you enjoy it, do your job well, and document your good work properly.

3. You'll learn how to communicate with people better, not only at work but also in your personal life.

4. Others around you will start to notice and decide they want to emulate your work. Passion is contagious.

You don't need to have rank in this job to help and lead others. I saw that early on in my career and always followed those whose work I admired. This book will motivate you to learn your job well, do it completely, get all the proper details, and then tell your story easily and efficiently.

All the best,
Mark

11

HOW AND WHY THE
FORMULA WORKS

In my conversations with officers, trainers, supervisors, and leaders across the country, the challenges of report writing keep coming up. There's still a lot of confusion about what details to include, how to structure their reports, and the finer points of grammar and punctuation.

However, the root of these issues often lies in motivation and mindset.

IT STARTS WITH INTRINSIC MOTIVATION AND MINDSET

I've noticed that some officers are reluctant to invest time in their reports, resulting in subpar work that gets kicked back by their supervisors. This cycle keeps officers and supervisors off the streets, compromises community safety, and leads to disappointing outcomes in court. The frustration builds, making the entire process feel overwhelming.

On the other hand, officers who are genuinely motivated to excel in their jobs and document their work properly tend to be the most successful.

That makes sense, right?

In my discussions with law enforcement leaders, we've identified high call volumes, insufficient supervisor review, and a lack of motivation to improve as significant challenges. However, there are officers who, despite being out in the field alone, rise to the occasion and achieve remarkable things.

The good news is that going above and beyond in this job isn't as hard as it might seem. Unfortunately, many officers settle for doing the bare minimum each shift. But why be one of those officers? Why not aim to be the officer whose reports are read by the FBI, DEA, or Secret Service? Imagine being the officer whose meticulous reporting helps put away drug smugglers, domestic violence offenders, or child predators for a long time.

Staying motivated is key. Every time you put on your uniform, I invite you to think about the bigger picture. The calls you respond to could be some of the most traumatic events in someone's life. Recognizing the importance of these moments and the role your reports play in addressing them can keep you motivated to do your best work.

When In Doubt, Follow the Formula

Imagine telling a seasoned golfer to change their swing and stance; it just wouldn't make sense. Instead, picture that golfer receiving a new set of clubs that enables them to hit the ball straighter and farther, all while reducing their time on the course.

If you're anything like me, you appreciate a good Formula for success. Following a proven Formula can lead to consistent victories, so who wouldn't want that? Here's some good news: I'm not asking you to overhaul your writing style.

As you keep reading, you'll continue to discover some simple adjustments that will significantly enhance your writing. However, the real win is the increased safety for you and your community that these changes can bring.

We'll dive deeper into these topics later, but it's impossible to cover everything here. That's why I encourage you to attend one of my classes (in person, live online, or on-demand).

Head over to PoliceReportFormula.com, sign up for my mailing list, and join the Report Sample Sharing Hub if you're an active law enforcement officer. You'll gain access to a wealth of report samples and have the chance to enroll in report writing workshops, and you can even request a review of your reports.

My Longer Story

Remember the young guy running down the street as his life depended on it?

I'll continue my story here.

After I turned my police car around to go and speak with the young man who had just been running down the sidewalk, I pulled up next to him. I asked him if everything was okay. He told me he had just gotten off a commuter bus but had left his brother's jacket onboard. He was still distraught, and he said he'd just call the bus company and see if he could get it back. I told the young man to jump into my car. We were going bus hunting.

As we were driving, he told me his brother had recently passed away. I instantly knew who he was. His name was Jack. His brother, Ben, was seventeen when he died from a rare form of cancer about six months prior. Ben's death hit our town hard. He was a star athlete at the local high school. Ben and Jack's father, Rob, had been our municipal prosecutor when I first started at my police department. I had known Rob for a long time. Unfortunately, the only other time I had met Jack was at his brother's wake. Our entire department went as a group.

NOTHING WAS GOING TO STOP US FROM FINDING THAT BUS.

We were able to catch up to the bus at an intersection. Shortly after the light turned green, I threw on my red and blue lights, and Jack was reunited with his brother's jacket. I then took Jack home. When I dropped him off, I could tell his whole spirit had been uplifted. That was all the reward I needed. I never told a soul about our encounter.

A week or so later, Jack's mom, Trish, posted a word of thanks on Facebook. Someone from a local news station saw the post, and our story ended up on

CBS News. This news story made some rounds and was seen by the Carroll family in Wisconsin. They sent me a touching letter, which you can read here.

Dear Sgt. Mark Tagliareni,

This year our family started thanking police officers. Our hope is to improve morale and let officers know they are appreciated. Furthermore, our goal is to thank officers in all 50 states and 3,142 counties in America.

Recently, we watched a video where you helped a young man find a jacket he left on a city bus. Your actions showed compassion, dedication, and commitment to helping those in need. Outstanding job, Sgt. Tagliareni! Thank you for being a police officer. The job you do matters and makes a huge difference in the greater good of our country.

The Carroll Family is committed to making an impact on people's lives. We hope our efforts serve as an example for others to express gratitude toward the brave men and women in their communities.

We are striving to improve morale amongst law enforcement personnel. In hopes of accomplishing this, we are asking people to share this Law Enforcement Challenge, refer a police officer to us, and thank the police in their communities. Together, we can impact people and our communities.

*Keep up the great work. May God bless you, your
family, and your department. Stay safe.*

*Thank you,
The Carrolls (Nate, Charlie, Louie, Millie)*

The Carroll family sent a letter to one officer in
every county in every state in America. It was an honor
to have received this letter as one of the 3,142 officers the Carroll family thanked (out of approximately
800,000 in our country).

What's the takeaway? Small actions don't go unno-
ticed and often have a huge impact. My own example is
something officers all over the country do every single
day. Be proud of the job you do. As you can see, it's
not just about good reports; it's about impact. And the
impact you make every day helps change the world.

This is the type of officer I was and the person I still
am. I cared deeply about my job and always wanted
to do it well. I cared deeply about my department
members and wanted the best for them.

MY CAREER WAS NOT ALWAYS FULL OF PROMISE AND POSITIVITY.

For the first eighteen years of my career, we had an
oppressive administration. One officer had little to
no empathy and was the "my way or the highway"
type of administrator. I quickly learned that you
could go with the flow and hopefully get promoted,
or you could push back against the various contract
and ethical violations and be written off. I was raised

to stand up for what was right. I couldn't watch this administrator treat officers the way he did, make us work one of the most insane schedules you could ever imagine (ask me about it), and destroy the department's morale.

I was our union president from 2006 to 2014. I initially felt that I could reason with the administrator and our township. I quickly realized the township was being misled by this administrator behind the scenes. I paid a price for standing up for the department, but I knew I was doing the right thing. All along, I always—well, almost always—stayed positive. I knew things would eventually change for the better, even if it took years.

I didn't want my inability to advance at work to get in the way of being a great cop. One of my friends and former co-workers, Mike Grassi, got me interested in criminal interdiction. Mike had worked for my department for a few years. He wound up transferring to a neighboring department for more opportunities. We stayed in touch, and he recommended that I take some training. As the years went on, I took as much training as I could in criminal interdiction. I eventually got pretty good at it. You may know this already, but not much tops the feeling of watching thousands of cars drive by you on a busy highway and being able to pick out one with occupants engaged in criminal activity.

As I was getting successful in making a lot of arrests, I was also under a microscope at work. I knew this administrator would take any chance to catch me making a mistake so he could potentially discipline me. I knew my reports had to be well-written with all the proper details.

The low point for my entire department came in 2015 and the beginning of 2016. It was also a tough time in my life. An officer who recently retired from our department passed away. He was only forty-nine. Our entire department came together with one exception. It was hard for a lot of us to fathom why this administrator stood separate from all other department members during the wake and funeral. I also lost a cousin who was only forty-eight. I remember standing in front of my locker in February 2016, wondering if things would ever get better. I hadn't been religious in quite a while up to that moment. However, I asked God to intervene. I was, and still am, a firm believer in karma.

Karma and Police Work

The administrator was forced to resign. By August 2016, I was promoted to sergeant. I had a great squad, and this allowed me to still be active in criminal interdiction. I had always been an excellent writer and knew I could put together a course on police report writing. The Formula I had developed was successful and easy to follow. I wanted to share it with the world. By always being positive, staying motivated, and knowing I could accomplish anything I put my mind to, I decided to apply to be a report writing instructor for a popular training company. I've been teaching cops to be better report writers since 2019. I hope to see you in one of my classes soon. In the meantime, use this book to change your mindset about report writing, stay motivated, and write best-in-class reports.

12

STEP 1 — PATROL BREATHING, MUSCLE MEMORY, AND ORIENTING YOUR MIND

We all develop muscle memory. If you do something enough, it will come naturally. That counts for both good habits and bad habits. When I had about six years on as a police officer, I responded to the scene of a hit-and-run auto accident. A pedestrian had been struck and was badly injured. The scene was chaotic. While on the scene, tending to the patient and preserving evidence, we received a call that the offender's vehicle had become disabled less than a mile from where we were located. (I promise not all my calls and successes dealt with disabled vehicles or pedestrians.) A few of us responded to the second scene.

We quickly realized the offender was intoxicated. He also happened to have only one hand. We later learned he had an accident when he was younger that caused part of his arm from the elbow down to be amputated. I started to put him through standardized field sobriety tests. As I was giving instructions, he kept putting his hand in his pocket. I kept saying, "Take your hands out of your pockets." My muscle memory had kicked in. I usually said this to people who had both hands. I was nervous; it was chaotic, and "Take your hands out of your pockets" came naturally.

If you do the same thing over and over, it becomes muscle memory. This is true for our current society, where texting is king. Not many of us use proper grammar, spelling, and punctuation when we text (me included). It's also been shown that so much texting leads to less social interaction. We have lost the ability to effectively communicate.

Am I saying to use good grammar and spelling when we text? No. However, it's important to truly care about proper writing skills when you are writing your police reports. Here's why you should care: Always remember that these reports are a direct reflection of you. You may be Super Cop out on the street, but if your reports are sloppy, that's how you'll be judged. And if you truly want to be Super Cop, writing good reports needs to be one of your superpowers.

How do you change your muscle memory when it comes to writing? You're going to love this. I would suggest typing your reports in programs such as Grammarly (an excellent program), MS Word, Google Docs, and Apple Pages, to name a few. As you type, pay attention to the editors built into these programs. Don't just let the program edit things for you. Pay attention to the suggestions the editor is making. Once your report is complete, copy and paste it into your records management system.

Why Every Word Counts

"The pen is mightier than the sword." You've probably heard that expression before. It was said by Edward Bulwer-Lytton, an English playwright. In policing, we have lots of tools in our arsenal. Sometimes, we are doctors, psychologists, mechanics, law enforcers, babysitters, and role models. The list goes on. No matter what we do at work and no matter what type of calls we are either sent on or initiate, we all write reports. More often than not, your written words will have longer-lasting effects than what you do on a daily basis.

Your words often guarantee convictions or acceptable plea bargains; they document why you were justified in the actions you took, and they sometimes describe the last moments of someone's life. I can list countless more examples of the importance of your written words.

Even though report writing is something we all do, when I ask people in class if they've taken any training in report writing since their basic academy class, the answer is usually no. If you want to be a great cop, you must realize that writing complete reports is all part of the Formula. Changing your mindset will lead to the results you want.

I recently spoke with someone in law enforcement who I admire greatly. Whenever I speak with him, I hear the passion in his voice. He is a constant learner and wants the best for his department and anyone he can help. One of his strengths is he is always looking to learn. During our conversation, he told me he has noticed that officers go on calls and get enough details to fill a four- to five-page report. Meanwhile, they are turning in reports that are four- to five-paragraphs long. We agreed that officers need to be more thorough and capture all the necessary details before they submit their reports.

ORIENTING YOUR MIND AND PATROL BREATHING

Fortunately, the stigma attached to officers being pro-active about mental health is decreasing. We have difficult and stressful jobs. I'm sure you're familiar with or have heard about different types of breathing and even meditation. For those of you who already incorporate daily breathing exercises or meditation into your routine, you know how beneficial they can be. As you start your shift, find someplace quiet to take three nice, long, deep breaths. Try to keep a small smile on your face as you do this.

This may sound silly, but I promise that over time, you will feel positive effects. Do this type of breath-ing—let's call it patrol breathing—whenever you have some downtime on your shift or even when respond-ing to a stressful call. Studies show that this activity has a tremendous impact on your parasympathetic nervous system. I know that's a big word and hard to pronounce, but trust me when it comes to this. The parasympathetic nervous system, also known as the involuntary nervous system, controls breathing and activates the body's relaxation response.

When someone is stressed, their body's sympathetic nervous system activates the fight-or-flight response, which can cause shallow breathing, rapid heartbeat, and anxiety. Slow, deep breathing can signal the parasympathetic nervous system to calm the body down and return it to a relaxed state. If you do this consistently over time, you will benefit now and in the future.

As you respond to a call, you are already formulating what actions you are possibly going to take. It's easy to fall into routines and handle similar calls in a similar fashion. We write up similar reports and move on to the next one. You must remember, though, that no matter how similar a call may be, they are all unique. Bring all your training and experience with you to each call, but remember, each experience will be different. If you strive to be a complete and well-rounded cop, show up to each call and be present.

Don't just go through the motions and assume your body camera recorded everything and then rely solely on your body camera to write your report. Later, I'll touch on body cameras again. By being present, caring, and empathetic at every call, you will be safer, more complete, and have all the details you need for a best-in-class report.

Now that I've hopefully changed your mindset about report writing, keep reading to learn the rest of the Formula to follow as you write.

13

STEP 2 — PAST TENSE, PLAIN LANGUAGE, AND THE ABCs

When I speak to students and answer questions on Facebook, a lot of officers ask if they should cite case law in their reports. The good news is you don't need to do this. Your job is to write in plain, simple language so the reader understands what happened. If you've covered all the important details (remember, by showing up and being a complete officer, you'll have all the details) and know your job well, your prosecutor can gain convictions and cite case law if needed. So, how do we write in clear and simple language? Think ABC and write in the past tense.

ABC - Accuracy, Brevity, and Completeness

From Accuracy to Impact: The Essentials

As I mentioned earlier, your mobile video recorder and body-worn cameras are great tools. However, they don't tell the whole story. Use these tools to tell your story accurately and in chronological order. Sometimes, it's hard to remember the exact order in which things took place. Your MVR and/or BWC will help with this. Watch the footage and use it to keep chronology and remember details that the camera may not have captured.

As I was doing research for this book, I spoke to officers who expressed concern that fellow officers were not accurate enough to let the reader know exactly what happened. This happens for a number of reasons. One example we discussed was when officers use force and try to sterilize the encounter. Officers will use phrases like, "I assisted the subject to the ground," when they actually tackled someone or used a takedown maneuver. If you tackled someone or used a takedown maneuver, say so. Make sure you're properly documenting the reasons you were forced to do this. Try to avoid using vague terms like "assisted someone to the ground" or "used a self-defense technique." Tell the reader exactly what you did and why you did it.

The Art of Balancing Detail and Brevity

What is brevity? It is the concise and exact use of words in writing or speech. This is something you'll fine-tune throughout your career. Early on, I think it's best to be overly detailed in your reports rather than under-detailed. As you improve this skill, try to use the right words to describe what happened. If you don't know the right word, please look it up. Officers tend to use lofty words or even the wrong words to sound more official. Try to write like you speak when having a conversation.

Here's a quick example: When was the last time you used the word ascertained when you spoke? If we were hanging out at a bar and I said, "I just ascertained that it costs $5 for each beer," you probably wouldn't want to hang out for long. As officers, we use words like ascertained in our reports a lot, but we never say them in conversation. You'll see a list of words like these and better alternatives to use in my class or by joining my mailing list. Keep it simple, and use plain language so any reader can understand what has happened.

The golden rule of editing is to remove one word from every sentence, one sentence from every paragraph, and one paragraph from every report. I know that sounds crazy, but you can accomplish this. Think of the sentence, "The girl said that she ate too much." Now, try it like this: "The girl said she ate too much." The word that is a filler word. It's often unnecessary. I'm guilty of using the word that too much in my writing.

How are you writing dialogue you've had with people? Is it something like this?

I asked the driver where he was coming from. He said Baker Street Mall. I asked him what stores he shopped at. He said he wasn't sure. I asked him if he bought anything at the mall. He said no. I asked if he made any stops along his route before I pulled him over. He said he stopped at a gas station. I asked him which gas station.

This type of writing is laborious for the reader.

What's the solution? I give you permission to paraphrase. Try this:

I asked the driver where he was coming from. He told me he had been at the Baker Street Mall. He wasn't sure what stores he had shopped at and didn't buy anything.

Practice eliminating unnecessary words and paraphrasing dialogue, and you'll write more efficiently.

TRANSFORMING YOUR SKILLS FROM BASIC TO BRILLIANT

You want to make sure you are complete when writing your reports. I've seen a lot of reports where the officer clearly leaves out details because he or she feels the body camera footage is enough. Is this truly being complete? No, it's far from it. A good defense attorney will realize you didn't cover an important detail. Maybe you're thinking that it's on your body cam, so you'll just talk about it on the stand if asked. A good defense attorney will make you look foolish for leaving something out of your report.

I love what one of my fellow instructors has to say about completeness. How many of you are watching all your body camera or mobile video recorder footage all the way through? Are you watching what the suspect said or did after you slapped on the handcuffs and secured them in the backseat of your car? If you're doing this, bravo! If not, absolutely start doing so. Guess what your arrestee is often doing or saying in your backseat on camera, things like, "Oh shit, I'm screwed," or, "I knew I shouldn't have drunk so much" (after they told you they only had two drinks.) Can these statements be included in your report? Absolutely. If you haven't seen any of Kenny Williams's front seat interviews and what the person in his front seat says and does when he isn't in his car, I encourage you to do so. It's powerful stuff.

KEEP IT IN THE PAST

When writing your reports, try to consistently write in the past tense. We are writing about events that have taken place in the past. Some editing programs won't catch verb tense errors. We'll talk about how to review reports later, but make sure you are not shifting from past to present tense as you write.

As I was researching this book, I came across an article about shifting verb tenses. According to the article, for most memoirists, past tense is best. We are pretty much memoirists. The article went on to say past tense makes logical chronological sense (we already talked about writing in chronological order), and it's usually the easiest verb tense to work with for the full duration of the manuscript. (The article can be found at MontanaCoauthor.com: "Writers Ask: Is it okay to switch between past and present tense?") In essence, we are writing memoirs every day, and the manuscripts are submitted to your supervisor for review. So, as the article points out, past tense is *easiest* to work with.

14

STEP 3 — THE TRUSTWORTHY AND ACTIVE VOICE

Receiving an email, text, or phone call from an unknown number or sender is like reading a report in third person or passive voice; you're not all that interested in it or trusting of it. I want my readers to be interested in what I write, and I want them to trust what they're reading. How do we accomplish this? Write your reports in the first person and write in an active voice.

I know there are some departments that still require their officers to write in the third person. If you work for one of these departments, perhaps you can encourage change. Examples of phrases in reports written in the third person are "this officer" or "Officer Summers responded" when you are Officer Summers. Third-person reports may even use labels like Suspect 1 or S1 or Victim 1 or V1. This gets confusing for your reader. If you want to be simpler and more straight-forward, write in first person. Use pronouns such as I, you, he, she, it, we, and me when writing your reports. It lets the reader know who is doing what.

Which sounds better?

"This officer responded to 123 Main St. on the report of a domestic in progress. Upon arrival, this officer spoke with Victim 1 in the living room of the residence."

—OR—

"I responded to 123 Main St. on the report of a domestic in progress. Upon my arrival, I spoke with Karen Simmons in the living room."

The second example is written in the first person, and this is what you should strive for in your reports.

Regarding active versus passive voice, if I could tell you one thing that will absolutely make your next report better, it is to write in an active voice. There is so much passive-voice writing in police reports. Many officers think passive voice makes their reports sound more official. Write your next report in an active voice, and I promise you'll love how it flows and how straightforward it comes out.

An active voice tells the reader who is doing the action. For example, "Billy picked up the brick and threw it out the window." Who's doing the action? Billy. Here's the same sentence written in a passive voice: "The brick was thrown out the window by Billy." I know it sounds too simple, and you may be asking yourself, "What's the big deal?" I promise if you write in an active voice, your next report will be better.

Here's an example you'll see in a lot of police reports: "The car was searched. During the search, a gun was located in the center console." Who's doing the action (searching)? Now, try it this way: "Officer Murphy and I searched the car. During our search, Officer Murphy located a gun in the center console." This tells the reader exactly who is doing the action. A report written completely in an active voice is much easier for you to write and for the reader to read. Go back over your past reports and look for passive-voice writing; you'll find it.

When you take my report writing class, we do interactive exercises with active and passive voice. These exercises help put things in perspective. If you are a brave soul and participate with a correct answer, you even win a prize. My class is offered in-person or on-demand. You'll have to attend in person if you want a shot at winning a prize, so check my website and look for when I'm teaching near you.

15

STEP 4 — WRITE LIKE A JOURNALIST, THE USE OF FORCE, AND IF YOU REMEMBER NOTHING ELSE

B e careful of subjectivity; use it sparingly and smartly because you don't want your reports influenced by personal feelings, tastes, or opinions.

In November 2014, I was working on a beautiful and unseasonably mild Sunday afternoon. I was watching traffic enter the highway from an on-ramp. After a while, a BMW with a large crack across its front windshield drove past me. The car was registered in Pennsylvania. The looks on the occupants' faces were hard to miss. There was a male driver, a male passenger, and a female in the back middle seat. She was sitting between two child seats. I later learned these child seats were occupied as well. I pulled out from my spot so I could stop the BMW.

As I followed, the driver committed a few more traffic violations. I also noticed that the female in the backseat kept looking over her shoulder to see where I was. After she looked back, she would turn and speak to the men in the front seats. I didn't know what she was saying, but as you read this, you can probably imagine what she was telling them.

Ask yourself: "In terms of your police report, what are the *facts* to report here?"

After following for about a mile, when I knew we were in a safe location, I pulled the car over. I told dispatch I was on a traffic stop, my location, and the vehicle's registration. Then, I approached the car on its passenger side. (As an aside, if you are stopping a lot of cars, make sure to use a passenger-side approach. There are so many reasons why this is safer for you.)

When I got to the front passenger window, I was greeted by the occupants. I could see that the two car seats were occupied by two young children, and I could smell both burnt and raw marijuana. I gathered the driver's documents and asked a few questions.

At one point, the driver, Jeff, told me it only took him forty minutes to get to his home in Pennsylvania (which was not possible unless he was driving 120 miles per hour). I had the driver step out of the car so I could speak with him alone.

(Here's another aside: If you want to be successful at criminal interdiction—and be safer—question people separately. You will pick up on disparities in their stories.)

After speaking with Jeff for a few minutes, I realized that his story did not make much sense. As we spoke, my sergeant arrived to back me up. I left Jeff with my sergeant and went to speak with the other two adult occupants. When I got back to the passenger side, I began speaking with the front-seat passenger. He had a big winter jacket on his lap, and he was clutching it tightly. He barely looked at me as I asked him questions. He kept staring straight ahead as if he hoped I would vanish.

Just the Facts

The male passenger's answers didn't match what the driver had told me, so I asked him to step out of the car. He was clutching his jacket strangely as if he was carrying something delicate. Considering it was a warm sixty degrees out, I found his grip on the jacket even more suspicious and asked him to leave it in the car. He carefully placed it on the passenger seat, trying not to disturb whatever was inside, which only raised my suspicions further. I directed him back to where my sergeant was handling the driver, Jeff.

When I picked up the jacket, expecting to find drugs, a two-toned semi-automatic handgun tumbled out onto the pavement. The shock of this discovery caused the woman in the backseat to start wailing. I drew my gun and alerted my sergeant as I secured the weapon underfoot, keeping both men covered until we could safely handcuff them.

After a thorough search, I found a holster wedged next to the driver's seat, a perfect fit for the handgun. It seemed likely the driver had been wearing the gun and passed it off to the passenger as I followed them. I noted this theory in my report—though in hindsight, I should have stuck strictly to the facts. Our search turned up two more loaded guns in the trunk, one in each man's backpack.

Years later, this situation unfolded in court, where the passenger, facing significant prison time due to a prior gun conviction, was acquitted. The defense used my speculative notes from the report against us, suggesting the passenger was merely an unwilling participant scared into hiding the weapon. The jury sided with this interpretation.

As I reflect on this, it's clear that while it was obvious to me all three knew about the guns, my role was to report only what I could factually substantiate, not my interpretations.

This experience underscored a crucial lesson in the importance of sticking strictly to the facts when documenting cases.

ACT LIKE A JOURNALIST

Your job as a police officer is to report the facts, just like a journalist. Keep your opinions out of reports. A well-written report will allow the reader to form the same opinion you have. For instance, if you and I were working together on the same squad and you came up and told me that someone was angry or nervous, I would believe you and probably have the same conclusion. However, it's not our job to give our opinions in our reports, like saying someone was nervous.

When documenting someone's behavior, it's crucial to be as detailed as possible. This practice allows you to paint an accurate picture of their state, whether they're angry, nervous, or under the influence. The more you focus on describing observable behavior, the clearer and more effective your reports will become. For instance, instead of simply stating your belief that Mr. Sumner was under the influence of opiates, describe the specific symptoms you observed: "Mr. Sumner was sweating profusely despite the cold weather; his pupils were unusually pinpoint and remained so, and there were fresh track marks visible on his arms."

When it comes to expressing opinions based on these observations, phrase them in a way that reflects your professional judgment without making unsubstantiated claims. You might say, "Based on my training and experience, I recognized that the symptoms displayed by Mr. Sumner, such as pinpoint pupils and excessive sweating, are commonly associated with opiate use." This approach suggests a professional inference rather than a definitive statement, maintaining objectivity and accuracy in your reporting.

THE USE OF FORCE

Talking about using force can be tough. No officer I know enjoys it. However, sometimes, to ensure everyone—including us—gets home safely, it has to happen. When you're in such a situation, it's crucial to detail not only how the individual was behaving but also how that affected you emotionally. Clear communication about these moments is essential.

For example, understanding body language and pre-attack indicators can be key. I recently attended a training where they talked about identifying signs that someone might be trained in physical combat. A common sign is a cauliflower ear, which usually comes from repeated blows to the ear like you might see in wrestling or boxing. If I encounter someone with cauliflower ears, it signals they likely know how to handle themselves in a fight. This knowledge can heighten my sense of caution.

Let's say I was interacting with Mr. Copeland, who suddenly started yelling and clenching his fists. I notice he has cauliflower ears, which tells me he might have combat training. Out of concern for my safety, I might prepare to use non-lethal force, like my OC spray, to ensure the situation doesn't escalate.

Sharing these observations isn't about making assumptions that someone is a criminal; it's about being prepared and understanding the risks. It's also about helping others reading your report understand why you felt threatened and why you chose to act as you did.

Remember, it's not just about what we feel but how we describe what we see. Instead of saying someone was "angry," describe their actions: yelling, spitting, veins bulging. These details offer a clear, factual account that supports your assessment.

For more tips on articulating these encounters, check out my website and consider joining my mailing list. You'll find plenty of real-life examples, like a report from an officer in Lawton, Oklahoma, who expertly described a dangerous situation that really brings to life the importance of detailed, observant reporting.

IF YOU REMEMBER NOTHING ELSE

One of the best things I've ever learned about reports came from a highly experienced lawyer in the NJ Attorney General's Office. His advice was to write one fact per sentence. I heard that and thought it was the perfect addition to *The Police Report Formula*.

In fact, it's really the formula *within* the Formula. Here are the benefits:

- You will avoid run-on sentences.

- You will avoid sentence fragments.

- Your sentences will be short and to the point.

- You won't commit as many grammatical errors.

- Your sentences will be more accurate and complete.

- You'll be more likely to stick to plain, simple language.

- Your reports will be full of simple facts that tell your reader exactly what happened.

If you want to see what this looks like in action, check out PoliceReportFormula.com. I have plenty of report examples that follow this "one fact per sentence" approach. This approach simplifies things, and you'll see how effective this formula within the Formula can be through real-life examples.

16

STEP 5 — A PRACTICAL GUIDE TO EFFECTIVE POLICE REPORTS

We all know the old saying, "If it ain't broke, don't fix it." Well, that applies to writing police reports, too. You've been learning the basics since grade school: Every report should have a beginning, middle, and end, also known as an introduction, body, and conclusion. Let's break it down.

INTRODUCTION

Sometimes, the introduction to a report can be a single paragraph, especially for straightforward calls like a burglar alarm—where you arrive, check the scene, find everything in order, and clear the call. However, for more complex situations, you might need a few paragraphs to set the scene.

For dispatched calls, it's crucial to include what the dispatcher relayed to you, setting the stage for what you expected versus what you encountered. For example, if dispatched to a reported assault at 123 Main Street, your report should begin with those details.

If I initiate a stop or call myself, I give a detailed account of why. Let's say I'm observing traffic and notice a vehicle with an equipment violation, which leads to a traffic stop. I'd detail my observations, such as the driver struggling to maintain lane discipline, which compounded the reasons for the stop.

BODY

This is where the meat of your report lives. You'll detail everything from your initial observations to the actions taken during the call. It's vital to gather as much information as possible—even if it seems excessive. It's better to have it and not need it than the other way around.

Use tools like body cameras to help keep your narrative accurate and chronological. They're invaluable for ensuring you don't miss or misremember details.

When making critical points, such as establishing reasonable suspicion or probable cause, isolate these in standalone paragraphs. This method emphasizes the rationale behind your actions clearly and concisely. For instance, if I arrest someone for driving under the influence, I bullet-point the specific reasons, like erratic driving, the smell of alcohol, and performance on sobriety tests, which directly support the arrest decision.

Conclusion

Wrap up your report definitively. If you made an arrest, specify the charges. If you handed off the case to detectives, state that. If evidence was secured, provide details of where it's stored. Your conclusion should leave no questions about the disposition of the incident.

Remember, clarity and detail are your allies in report writing. By structuring your reports with clear introductions, detailed bodies, and concise conclusions, you ensure your documentation is thorough, understandable, and useful for anyone who might rely on it later.

17

THE ART OF THE POLICE REPORT REVIEW

When you're finished writing your report, remember: you're not done!

It's crucial to take the time to proofread your reports. No matter how sophisticated your writing tools are, they won't catch every mistake. Remember, your report reflects your professionalism. Any overlooked typo or error can undermine your credibility.

Always start by proofreading on your computer to catch initial mistakes. Then, print your report and take another look. Sometimes, you catch different errors on paper. Also, stepping away for a brief break before you review can help refresh your perspective and improve your focus when you return.

I always recommend having a colleague glance over your work. It's easy to read what you meant to write instead of what's actually on the page. I've shared some of my reports with missed typos on my website as examples. Once your report gets the all-clear from a peer, you're good to go.

A Note to Supervisors

If you're in a supervisory role, it's your responsibility to thoroughly review the reports submitted by your team. We've all seen supervisors who rush through approvals at the end of a shift. Remember, your name is on that report, too, alongside the officer who wrote it. By giving each report the attention it deserves, you not only uphold quality standards but also provide valuable feedback that can help officers improve over time. This commitment can lead to better reports and more efficient field supervision, creating a win-win situation for everyone involved.

18

WRAPPING IT UP

Thank you for taking the time to read through this guide. We've come to the end, but really, it's just the beginning. You've seen how changing your mindset can enhance your effectiveness from the start of your report to the end. We've dispelled common myths about police reporting, emphasizing how vital good reporting is—not just for bureaucracy but for saving lives and delivering justice.

You've learned how interconnected our actions and words can be. What might seem minor at first can have significant implications down the line. The practices outlined here aim to assist you whether you're new to the force or a seasoned veteran, and they're particularly supportive for those who might face language barriers or learning challenges.

To all the report writing instructors, field training officers, and heads of academies: You now have a resource to bolster your training programs and ensure your trainees are well-equipped to write effectively.

THE POLICE REPORT FORMULA

This book isn't just a training manual; it's an invitation to join a community that values quality policing and communication. Keep in touch, stay motivated, and keep improving.

Warm regards,
Mark

P.S. Make sure you visit PoliceReportFormula.com and join my mailing list. Just click on the "Subscribe" tab right on the home page, or scroll to the bottom of the homepage and fill out the "Subscribe Form."

To get access to report samples and the other website groups, please visit PoliceReportFormula.com and click on "Report Sample Sharing Hub and Groups." Once vetted for membership, you'll have access to many police report samples, writing tips, and tools and belong to a community of learners and people who want to serve justice better.

www.ingramcontent.com/pod-product-compliance
Lightning Source LLC
Chambersburg PA
CBHW021533260326
41914CB00001B/9